HOW OUR CHOICES IMPACT EARTH™

RECYCLING AND YOU

NICHOLAS FAULKNER
AND STEPHANIE WATSON

rosen publishing's
rosen central®
New York

Published in 2019 by The Rosen Publishing Group, Inc.
29 East 21st Street, New York, NY 10010

First Edition

Library of Congress Cataloging-in-Publication Data

Names: Faulkner, Nicholas, author. | Watson, Stephanie, 1969– author.
Title: Recycling and you / Nicholas Faulkner and Stephanie Watson.
Description: New York : Rosen Central, 2019. | Series: How our choices impact Earth | Includes bibliographical references and index. | Audience: Grades 5–8.
Identifiers: LCCN 2017050840| ISBN 9781508181538 (library bound) | ISBN 9781508181545 (pbk.)
Subjects: LCSH: Recycling (Waste, etc.)—Juvenile literature.
Classification: LCC TD794.5 .F38 2019 | DDC 363.72/82—dc23
LC record available at https://lccn.loc.gov/2017050840

Manufactured in the United States of America

CONTENTS

INTRODUCTION

Believe it or not, people didn't invent recycling. Converting waste into reusable materials is as old as Earth itself. Yes, nature is the perfect recycler. When an organism dies, its remains are converted into other substances that can be reused by other organisms. When those organisms die, the process starts all over. In the end, nature produces zero waste.

Humans can learn a lot from nature. Much of what we create produces a lot of waste. Those sneakers you outgrow, that iPhone you're trading in for the latest model, or even that banana peel you toss in the trash, are often left to pile up. In 2016, the average amount of trash each American produced daily was 4.4 pounds (2 kilograms).

When you roll the garbage bin out to the curb once or twice every week, a garbage truck picks it up and takes it to a transfer station. From there, most garbage goes to a landfill—a large deep area in the ground where trash is deposited, layer upon layer. And those landfills keep growing bigger. You don't have to worry about trash piling up on your street, which is good news. The bad news is that sticking tons and tons of waste in a landfill means that all those pieces of garbage can never be used again. One day, there won't be any more space to put our trash. As of 2016, America had more than two thousand active landfills and thousands of inactive ones.

Plastics, especially, are a major problem. According to National Geographic, in 2017, 91 percent of plastics weren't being recycled. And ever since

Much of the trash we throw away on a regular basis can be recycled. Sorting facilities can sift out materials that can be converted into new products.

plastic was first manufactured sixty years ago, we've generated 9.1 billion tons (8.3 billion metric tons) of it. Given that plastics can take up to four hundred years to break down, we're going to have much more of it accumulate if we don't fix the problem.

Recycling is an easy solution, and it's growing more popular with each coming year. Most communities have recycling programs to make the process easy. All you have to do is sort your used items and a truck will pick them up and take them to a recycling center. Sometimes you can even earn money by turning in used bottles and cans.

And recycling is not the only solution. You can also reuse. Turning something old and unneeded into something new and useful is the idea behind reuse. What if, instead of throwing away all those old items, you turned them into something else? What if you used your old food scraps to make fertilizer for your garden or flower bed?

The best solution, though, by far, is to simply reduce our consumption. Not only does that reduce waste, it also cuts down on the pollutants that are created in the manufacturing and shipping of goods.

CHAPTER ONE

RECYCLING ESSENTIALS

Recycling is an essential part of living on this planet. If Mother Nature never recycled, there would be piles and piles of the remains of plants and animals rising to the sky. People have to recycle, too, or our waste will accumulate to the point where it's no longer manageable. To avoid towering skyscrapers of piled-up trash everywhere, people have come up with a variety of ways to dispose of the vast amounts of garbage they produce. The three main methods for getting rid of trash are landfills, incineration, and recycling.

Most of the trash produced by households goes into large landfills (also called dumps). Garbage that is collected from one town or city is transported by truck or train to a great big hole in the ground. Waste is released into sections of the landfill called cells. About 2 feet (.6 meters) of wet clay is put down and fills itself in as it settles over time. Thick plastic is laid over the clay. About 8 feet (2.4 meters) of waste is placed in each cell and is then covered with about 6 inches (15.2 cm) of soil, called daily cover. Another layer of garbage is added, followed by another layer

Landfills, or dumps, are usually out of sight. However, looking at one can really open your eyes to how much trash we produce.

of dirt, and so on. The capping, or top cover, of the cell is sloped so that precipitation will not collect on the top. Finally, grass is planted over the top cover. Filling a landfill is like making a layer cake—although a very dirty, smelly one.

It's obvious that garbage isn't clean. Many of the items thrown in the trash contain toxic chemicals, which could drain into the water supply or get into the air. (Toxic waste must be disposed of at a hazardous waste site. It is illegal to dump toxic waste at a landfill for household waste.) When these chemicals combine, they produce a liquid substance called leachate. Landfills for household waste have barriers that help slow down the leachate from getting out. The bottom of the landfill is lined with compacted clay, which is then covered with a thick plastic liner. The plastic liner is not supposed to break down and is made to last a long time. (Currently, some researchers believe that liners delay the process of the leachate flowing out and contaminating groundwater but they do not prevent it from doing so. Usually the liner is checked for any leakage.)

Landfills also have special drainage systems—pipes and valves that collect liquid runoff and send it to a treatment plant. At the treatment plant, toxic chemicals and heavy metals are removed. The remaining liquids are cleaned and purified, and they are then returned to the water supply.

Chemicals in landfills aren't just in liquid form. Sometimes, they can be released into the air as gas. As garbage is exposed to sun, rain, and air, it decomposes (breaks down) and releases methane gas, which can be dangerous to the environment and can easily catch fire. Landfills have special systems in place to monitor and control how much methane gas is produced. Many landfills capture methane gas and convert it into energy.

The second method of removing waste is called incineration. Incineration can help reduce the amount of trash put in landfills. Waste is burned in a machine called an incinerator. The first incinerator was built in 1885 on Governor's Island in New York Harbor. By the early twentieth century, cities had begun using their trash incinerators to produce energy.

Even though incineration is an effective way to destroy trash and create energy, it is not used as often as it once was. The reason, in part, is because of concerns that burning trash can release harmful chemicals into the air. Today, only about 20 percent of solid waste is incinerated, according to the EPA.

Recycling—making garbage into something new so that it can be used again—is the third method for getting rid of trash. Just about everything, from soda cans to newspapers, printer cartridges to iPhones, can be recycled. Sometimes, an item made from recycled products becomes more valuable than the original product. New York City artist Justin Gignac sells plastic cubes filled with New York City garbage. He charges up to $100 for each garbage cube. Designers are creating clothing and jewelry out of fibers taken from recycled textiles. These pieces often cost more than the original garments from which they were made.

JOINING THE COMMUNITY

Should people be required to recycle or should they be able to choose whether or not they do? The answer to that question depends on where in the nation you live. Some communities have mandatory recycling—laws or ordinances that require people to recycle. Which products are recycled depends on the local laws, but people who refuse to recycle must pay a fine.

Most communities today have recycling programs that allow you to sort your trash into recyclable and nonrecyclable goods.

Other areas of the country have voluntary recycling programs, in which people are encouraged, but not required, to recycle. One of the ways communities encourage recycling is with pay-as-you-throw programs. These programs charge people for trash pickup based on the amount of garbage they throw away. For example, a 12-gallon (45.4-liter) trashcan may cost $10 per month for pickup, whereas a 32-gallon (121-liter) trashcan costs $30 per month. People who are part of this program want to recycle because it saves them money on their trash.

CRITICAL PERSPECTIVES

For perspective, some critics argue that recycling isn't all it's cracked up to be. Here's what they have to say:

- Landfill space is abundant. US landfills are nowhere near holding their capacity—there is still room to hold all the trash this country makes, and more. A. Clark Wiseman, an economist at Gonzaga University in Spokane, Washington, once calculated that all the trash that the United States creates by the year 3000 could fit in a square piece of land 100 yards (91.4 m) deep and 35 miles (56.3 km) wide on each side.
- Landfills are safe. Modern landfills have so many precautions in place, from plastic liners to drainage systems, that some experts say there is no risk of any chemicals escaping.
- Recycling uses energy and creates pollution. Extra trucks are needed to pick up recycling and drop it off at processing facilities. It takes energy to produce new goods from recycled ones. Both processes of picking up recyclables and turning them into new products release pollution into the air.
- Recycling is expensive. It often costs city recycling programs more to pick up and sort bottles, cans, and other products than the cities receive when they sell those items to manufacturers.

- **People recycle more than they can use. Recycling has become so popular that some products are in abundant supply. For example, the United States sells much of its recycled paper to China because there aren't enough uses for all that paper in the United States.**
- **Recycling does not work forever. Many items cannot be recycled over and over again. Paper, for example, will wear out after being recycled a few times. Eventually manufacturers will have to cut down more trees and find other raw materials. Recycling does not save resources forever—it just delays their use.**

The arguments both for and against recycling are likely to continue in the years to come. In the future, it will be up to you and your peers to decide what to do with your garbage.

Which is more effective, voluntary or mandatory recycling? According to the US Department of Energy, mandatory programs are more successful. About half of the people in mandatory programs recycle, compared to only one-third of the people in voluntary programs.

RECYCLING HELPS

The biggest benefit of recycling and reusing is that they reduce the amount of trash that goes into landfills. Yet recycling didn't eliminate all the garbage being thrown away.

The United States is a big country, but it still has to house more than 323 million people—and their trash. As cities expand, space for landfills becomes harder to find. Space that is available isn't always usable because people don't want landfills close to their homes and schools.

The reason why people don't want to live near landfills is that they are often full of chemicals, such as pesticides, paint thinners, and battery acid. Although safeguards are in place to help keep those chemicals from getting into the air and water supply, some health experts say the safeguards aren't perfect. A few studies have found that people who live close to landfills have a higher risk of getting cancer than people living farther away.

Landfills also aren't free. Garbage companies must pay a tipping fee to dump their trash. The tipping fee is based on the weight of the garbage. The trash company must pass the cost along to its customers.

In addition to saving landfill space, there are other benefits to recycling. Recycling saves natural resources. It conserves trees, which are essential to the environment because they pull carbon dioxide gas from the air. Carbon dioxide is a major contributor to global warming.

Trash costs money. The companies that run your garbage trucks charge a fee for bringing trash to landfills.

Recycling can reduce air and water pollution. It helps keep chemicals and toxic trash out of landfills. Recycling also reduces the amount of pollutants released during the manufacture of new products. Recycling 1 ton (0.9 metric ton) of steel prevents 200 pounds (90.7 kg) of air pollutants, 100 pounds (45.4 kg) of water pollutants, and almost 3 tons (2.7 metric tons) of mining waste from being released, according to Harvey Blatt in *America's Environmental Report Card.*

Recycling saves energy. It takes a lot more energy to find raw materials, make a new product, and then dispose of it than it does to recycle an old product. Recycling one aluminum can, for example, uses 95 percent less energy than making new aluminum out of ore, says the EPA.

Recycling creates jobs. Businesses are able to create and sell many new products that are made using recycled materials. Overall, recycling is a great idea. Yet believe it or not, there are also many convincing reasons people give for not recycling.

CHAPTER TWO

WHAT CAN BE RECYCLED?

A lot of household trash is recyclable. We just don't always realize it. Once we become knowledgeable about what can and can't be recycled, we have the ability to make smarter choices that can benefit our environment.

Recycling begins at the curb outside your house. You put your recyclables—plastic bottles, aluminum cans, and paper—into one bin or separate them into individual bins. About once each week, a truck comes by to pick up those items. Some recycling trucks have separate containers to hold each type of recyclable. Other trucks combine all the recyclables together and the trash company separates them at a processing facility.

Curbside pickup isn't the only way to collect recycling. There are other methods for disposing of your recyclable goods. Drop-off centers are places where you can bring your own recycling. These facilities accept everything from paper and bottles to hazardous materials, such as batteries or paint. Although drop-off centers save money on pickup costs, people such as you have to make the effort to bring your recyclables there.

Many states offer a small refund for your empty bottles. While not much money, these pennies can add up.

Deposit/refund programs pay people a cash refund (usually five or ten cents) for dropping off their bottles or aluminum cans. People can either visit a bottle collection facility or use a reverse vending machine (often found at supermarkets), which accepts empty bottles and cans and dispenses cash (or a refund receipt) in exchange. Not every state requires that companies put a refundable deposit on bottles and cans. Only about eleven states currently have these "bottle bills."

Buy-back centers pay cash for your old aluminum, scrap metal, glass, plastics, and newspapers.

Volunteer pickup is when community organizations (such as the Boy Scouts or a church group) raise money by collecting recyclable goods and bringing them to bottle collection facilities or buy-back centers.

As these programs illustrate, there are many ways to handle recycling. Some of them even reward you with money for your efforts.

THE RECYCLING PROCESS

No matter where they are picked up, when recyclable goods arrive at a processing facility, they are separated. From there, each item takes a different journey.

Aluminum cans are the most recycled type of container. Aluminum recycling is very efficient because it uses 95 percent less energy than making new aluminum. To recycle aluminum, used cans are crushed and the labels are burned off in a very hot oven called a furnace. Then the aluminum is melted, and the molten aluminum is poured into barlike shapes called ingots. These ingots are rolled into flat sheets and stretched very thin. Most old aluminum cans are used to make new aluminum cans, but they also can be made into objects like car parts, tin foil, and pie plates.

Paper is sorted by color, weight, type (newspaper, boxes, writing paper), and whether it has already been recycled. Then it goes into a big, hot bath filled with chemicals and water, which breaks the paper down into fibers. After a while, the paper turns into a souplike mush, called pulp. The pulp goes through a filter, which

Paper-recycling facilities can handle a huge amount of all different types of paper products, such as newspapers, magazines, and old books.

removes staples and glue. Chemicals pull the ink off the paper in a process called deinking. The pulp may also be bleached with hydrogen peroxide or chlorine to turn it white. Then it is rolled through a big machine into flat sheets. The sheets are heated, dried, pressed, and wound onto a giant roll. Finally, the roll is cut into sheets of new paper, which is used to make newspapers, tissue, boxes, packaging, and more paper.

Plastics aren't recycled as often as paper and aluminum because they are very inexpensive to produce. Only about one out of every four bottles is recycled, according to the Washington State Department of Ecology. When plastic is recycled, it is first sorted by color and type of plastic. You can tell what type of plastic it is by looking at the bottom of the bottle or package. The recycling code number is inside a triangle made of arrows (the universal recycling symbol). After the plastic is sorted, it is chopped up into tiny pieces and melted. Recycled plastics can be made into things like new furniture, insulation, construction materials, lunch trays, and egg cartons.

UNDERSTANDING THE CODES

The next time you get a plastic bottle, turn it over and look for the universal recycling symbol and the code on the bottom. Then compare it to the chart below to see what type of plastic was used to make it. These codes don't necessarily mean that all the plastics can be recycled—they only identify the type of plastic. Types 1 and 2, for example, are widely used in container form.

Type 4 is sometimes used in bag form. Types 6 and 7 have almost no recycling potential and are harmful to your health and the environment, according to the handbook *Greenopia*.

Code	Type of Plastic	Used in These Products
1	Polyethylene terephthalate (PET or PETE)	Soda bottles, peanut butter jars, water bottles
2	High density polyethylene (HDPE)	Milk and water jugs, juice bottles, shampoo bottles, toys
3	Polyvinyl chloride (PVC or V)	Detergent/cleanser bottles, pipes
4	Low density polyethylene (LDPE)	Soda six-pack rings, sandwich bags, plastic wrap, grocery bags
5	Polypropylene (PP)	Margarine tubs, straws, syrup bottles, yogurt cups, diapers
6	Polystyrene (PS)	Styrofoam packing peanuts, egg cartons, foam cups
7	Multi-layer plastics	Ketchup and baby bottles, food storage containers

Glass can be recycled, but not all types of glass can be easily used again. Window, mirror, and light bulb glass are too expensive to recycle, so usually only glass from jars and bottles is recycled. When glass bottles are collected, they are sorted by color and ground into very tiny bits called cullet. Other substances, such as limestone, sand, and soda ash are added to the cullet, and then the mixture is melted down and formed into new glass. Most glass bottles contain at least 25 percent recycled glass, according to the Washington State Department of Ecology.

Steel is recycled from old cars and buildings. US laws require that all steel used in manufacturing contains at least some recycled steel. Old cars and building materials are shredded, melted, and then rolled into huge sheets or coils. Everything from railroad ties to new cars can be made from recycled steel.

Even items as big as cars can be recycled. Huge crushing machines flatten them to the point where they're little more than blocks of metal.

Even scrap steel from the World Trade Center has been recycled. After terrorists struck the twin towers on September 11, 2001, steel from the two buildings was melted down and forged to make the bow (forward part) of the military ship the USS *New York*.

Tires are difficult to recycle because the rubber used to make them goes through a process called vulcanization. This process makes tires bouncy and springy, but it also makes the rubber harder to melt down. To recycle tires, companies have to first shred them into strips. Powerful magnets pull out any metal that is inside the tires. Then the strips are fed into a machine that grinds them into small pieces. Used tires can be used in manufacturing things such as playground surfaces, doormats, doorstops, and garden hoses.

Batteries often contain toxic chemicals such as lead, mercury, and nickel, which can be very dangerous if they are released into the environment. That's why most states require people to recycle batteries—especially car batteries. Different types of batteries have their own recycling process. Lead batteries, for example, are placed into a machine called a hammermill, which crushes them into pieces about the size of a nickel. The pieces are placed into a tank where they are separated by weight. The heavier pieces (lead) sink to the bottom, while the lighter pieces (rubber and plastic) float to the top. Each of these materials is then treated separately. Lead is melted in furnaces and poured into molds. It is cooled and then shipped to manufacturers to be used in new batteries. Plastic, often used in car

HOW MUCH TRASH DO YOU THROW AWAY?

If you're like the average American, you toss more than four pounds (just under two kilograms) of garbage every day of the year. That's just you—one person. Add in the more than 323 million people living in this country, and it amounts to 258 million tons (234 metric tons) of garbage produced each year, according to the latest US Environmental Protection Agency's (EPA) Facts and Figures from 2014. In that same year, 89 million tons (80.7 metric tons) of garbage were recycled and composted, which means we only have a 34.6 percent recycling rate.

This figure merely scratches the surface of all the trash in the United States. Add to it food scraps, junk mail, cell phones, bicycles, books, and literally thousands of other consumer goods, and you can see why the country is dealing with a whole lot of trash.

Imagine if all the trash created every year were just piled up on the street. It would stretch high into the sky, creating skyscrapers of garbage. The smell from rotten food and waste products would be overpowering.

battery covers, is recycled just like other types of plastic. A special chemical is added to battery acid to turn it into a harmless mixture of water and salt. Once it has been tested to make sure it is safe, the recycled acid is sent into the public sewer system.

Electronic waste, or e-waste, is becoming a growing area of the recycling industry. Consider all the electronics you have in your home: cell phones, iPads, TV sets, video games, and more. Now multiply those items by the millions of households in the United States. Finally, consider how often you replace each of your electronics and buy new products. A statistic from the organization Keep America Beautiful reveals that the average person gets a new computer every three to five years. That means hundreds of millions of computers turn into junk every year. You can't just throw out electronics because many of them are made with toxic materials, such as lead, nickel, and mercury. You can donate electronics that still work to schools and

While electronic devices make our lives more convenient and connected, they also make a lot of waste that needs to be recycled.

nonprofit organizations. Manufacturers will often accept broken electronics. They will take the electronics apart and use many of the pieces (including batteries, plastic handsets, and circuit boards) to make new products.

THE VALUE OF REUSE

Reusing old items is another way to prevent them from winding up in landfills. The idea behind reuse is to find a new home—or purpose—for something that's no longer needed. Some of the ways companies and individuals reuse include the following:

- Using building scraps and unused construction materials to make houses for people who can't afford a place to live. Some builders use recycled denim for insulation and reclaimed wood for flooring. Some architects are even converting old steel shipping containers into housing.
- Donating unused canned goods to food banks, where they go to feed the hungry.
- Giving used furniture to Goodwill or a thrift store so other people can buy it at low cost.

Donation drives are a great way to make sure your unused canned goods don't go to waste. They also help the hungry.

- Providing unused art supplies to schools that lack supplies.
- Dropping off clothing at a consignment store so you can make money on items you no longer use.
- Donating gently used or never used toys to churches or organizations that give these gifts to less fortunate families during the holidays.

Reuse is a win-win situation. It helps people and companies that no longer need their old products clear out clutter while providing much-needed goods to people who can really use them.

CHAPTER THREE

RECYCLING, YESTERDAY AND TODAY

Today, we are more aware than ever about the importance of recycling. Every day, we see messages on the internet and social media, encouraging us to be more environmentally friendly. Though recycling and reuse may seem like new ideas, they've been around for millions of years. In fact, the biggest recycler and reuser of all is nature. When plants and animals die, they are absorbed into the ground or oceans. Those decomposing bodies provide nourishment for the next generation of plants and animals.

Humans got into the act of recycling much later. Around 200 BCE, the Chinese found a new use for old fishing nets—they created the world's first recycled paper. The ancient Maya used to recycle entire buildings. Instead of tearing down old buildings and starting from scratch, they simply added on to existing structures.

The US government began to get actively involved in recycling during the twentieth century. During World War I (1914–1918) and World War II (1939–1945), soldiers needed a constant flow of weapons, clothing, and other goods at the European front. The American

Today, recycling is a common practice. However, it took many years to get to this point, and it will take many more to eliminate waste altogether.

government encouraged people to collect everything from newspapers to aluminum to help the military effort. The motto during World War I was "Don't Waste—Save It."

In 1965, the US population had grown to more than 193 million and the number of consumer goods being used—and thrown away—rose. That year the government passed the Solid Waste Disposal Act to help manage the country's growing trash problem. In 1976, the act was renamed the Resource and Conservation and Recovery Act. It set up national standards for treating and storing waste. The act also emphasized conservation, in part by encouraging people and companies to recycle.

The recycling revolution really got going on April 22, 1970, when Senator Gaylord Nelson of Wisconsin started the very first Earth Day celebration. One day each year, Americans would gather for festivals and rallies to promote environmental awareness and find ways to protect the planet. Recycling played a big part in this annual celebration, which helped launch the US Environmental Protection Agency (EPA). Today the EPA oversees recycling efforts across the country and sets goals for recycling more of the trash people use. In 1988, the EPA announced a five-year goal to recycle 25 percent of trash. By 2014, Americans were recycling just under 35 percent of their garbage.

The United States still does not have a national recycling law. However, many states have established their own laws requiring residents to recycle. Some states have passed laws that pay people back a five- or ten-cent deposit when they return bottles and cans. Eleven states—including California, Oregon, Connecticut, Massachusetts, Michigan, and New York—currently have these bottle and can recycling laws. Some cities and states have laws that prevent people from throwing away recyclable items. If you live in New York City, for example, you can be fined $25 for mixing recyclables in with your regular trash.

CHANGING THE WORLD ON A LOCAL LEVEL

Although recycling isn't the law across the country, local communities, religious organizations, and schools have stepped in and started programs of their own. The following are just a few of the community-based recycling programs that have made a difference.

School lunch tray recycling program. Many schools recycle paper and aluminum cans, but one Georgia school district took recycling a step further. When the Gwinnett County Public School system discovered that

REDUCE, REUSE, RECYCLE

Recycling is just one part of the "three Rs"—reduce, reuse, and recycle. All of the "Rs" represent ways to conserve natural resources.

"Reduce" means using less by choosing products that are long lasting. Instead of eating your dinner on disposable plates and then throwing them away, you use regular dishes and wash them when you're finished. Rather than packing your lunch in a brown paper bag, you bring the same lunchbox or canvas bag to school every day. You can also bring a reusable cup instead of using and throwing away disposable cups.

"Reuse" means finding another use for items instead of throwing them away. You might donate your old sunglasses to a charity or have your broken computer fixed so that you don't have to trade it in for a new one.

"Recycle" means turning materials you're no longer using into something you can use. You could recycle old newspapers to be turned into new newsprint or give your empty soda cans to a recycling center so that they can be melted down and turned into new cans. Unlike reuse, recycling breaks down old products into raw materials, which are then made into new items.

it was sending more than sixteen million polystyrene plastic lunch trays to landfills each year, it came up with a plan to collect and recycle the trays. In its first year, the program recycled more than six million lunch trays.

Recyclebank. Ron Gonen cofounded Recyclebank over a decade ago in Philadelphia, Pennsylvania. The idea was to encourage people to recycle by offering them something valuable in return. When people recycle through Recyclebank, they earn points, which can be used to buy products at hundreds of different stores.

Recycling lottery. In the city of Rockford, Illinois, residents have a good reason to recycle—a big cash prize. One homeowner's trash is selected by chance each week and checked. If no recyclable items are found,

Recyclebank cofounder Ron Gonen (*right*) has worked with New York City to expand curbside collection of organic materials.

the homeowner wins $1,000. If the person selected doesn't win, the lottery goes up to $2,000 the next week, $3,000 the following week, and so on. After a few months of launching this lottery, Rockford had a 400 percent increase in recycling!

Putting computers to good use. One company is doing something good with old computers. The Assistive Technology Exchange Network in Illinois collects computers from companies that no longer need them and donates them to children who have disabilities.

Giving prom dresses a second life. When Shauna Cole, director of the Teen Program at the Reston Community Center in Reston, Virginia, found out that many local high school girls couldn't afford prom dresses, she came up with the perfect solution. Shauna started collecting prom dresses, shoes, jewelry, and makeup from people all over northern Virginia. The center's Prom Dress Giveaway collected five hundred dresses in its first year, giving hundreds of girls an unforgettable prom night.

A GLOBAL PHENOMENON

The United States is getting better about recycling, but other countries have come up with their own unique ways of making sure their trash doesn't wind up in landfills.

In Switzerland, for example, recycling is free, but trash is expensive. Supermarkets collect bottles, towns pick up paper and yard waste, and aluminum and tin can be dropped off at local depots at no charge. Yet for each bag of trash residents put out for collection, they must pay 1.50 in Swiss Francs (about $1.30).

Toy cars made from old cans and other types of packaging are on display in Madagascar. This is a great way to reuse discarded materials.

In Bali, Indonesia, people don't just take used bottles to a recycling center. They wash them by hand and then refill them with drinks themselves.

In East Africa, people use old cans and other used items to make toys and fix the roofs on their homes.

In Germany, people collect their recyclables in at least five different bins: packaging, paper, glass, food waste, and other types of trash. Each bin has a different color to make sorting easy.

THE SCIENCE OF RECYCLING

The idea behind recycling is pretty basic: put your used bottles, cans, and paper out by the curb and a truck picks them up to be taken to a processing plant. Traditional recycling is just one part of the picture, though. As technology gets more advanced, science is coming up with new ways to recycle and reuse.

One of those ways is to produce products that will be biodegradable (break down) more quickly in landfills. It's an idea called green chemistry. An example is that of plastic. Most plastics are not very biodegradable. If you throw out a plastic cup, it can sit in a landfill for hundreds of years without breaking down. One company, SpudWare, is helping to solve that problem by making plastic out of something people normally eat: potatoes. The company's forks and knives are made from 80 percent potato starch and 20 percent soy oil, which break down in about six months. Utensils and plates can also be made from corn, cassava, and sugarcane.

The Edible Spoon Maker machine "bakes" dough into the shape of a spoon, which can be used for eating as well as eaten.

Today many companies start thinking about how their products might break down before they even build those products. The idea is called design for disassembly. For example, before home builders construct a new house, they look at all the pieces that will go into that house—windows, doors, flooring, carpets, and so on. The builders try to use the fewest number of parts and materials possible, and then they figure out how each of the pieces used to make the house can one day be reused, recycled, or safely thrown away.

Another new idea in recycling is to turn garbage into something usable—such as fuel or fertilizer. A few companies are testing a method for turning wood chips into ethanol, a type of alcohol that can be used to power cars. Almost any type of material containing hydrogen, carbon, and oxygen—from garbage to leftover farm crops—could potentially be turned into fuel because these products release energy when they are burned. A few seafood companies are even turning old fish parts into fertilizer. With creative ideas like these, the recycling possibilities are virtually endless.

MYTHS & FACTS

Myth: Recycled items are always worth less than the original products.
Fact: Although you may get only five cents for the bottle of soda that cost you one dollar, some recycled goods are actually worth more than what was paid for them. For example, some artists charge thousands of dollars for paintings and sculptures they have made out of garbage.

Myth: Dumping trash in landfills costs less than recycling.
Fact: Sometimes that is true because it can cost more to pick up, separate, and process recyclables than it costs to dump them in a landfill. However, when recycling programs are done right, they can actually be cheaper than landfills. It costs a lot less to recycle most old items than it costs to find the raw materials and make a whole new product, according to the EPA. Furthermore, the more people who recycle, the less expensive recycling programs will become.

Myth: You can't reuse disposable items.
Fact: Anything can be reused, even products that were designed to be used only once. For example, once you've finished your soda, you can save the can, cut it up, and make a piece of art. Or, you can string together the soda tabs to make a belt. Instead of throwing away your empty Styrofoam cup, you can plant flower seeds in it.

CHAPTER FOUR

DOING YOUR PART

While recycling may be more popular than ever, so is consuming stuff. Never before has it been so easy to purchase products online. You just go to your favorite shopping website and click a button. A few days later—or even a few hours later—your item arrives like a gift. But all this stuff just adds up and eventually becomes waste.

If you're like most young people, your house is full of stuff. You have books you no longer read, clothes you've outgrown, and toys you no longer play with. What should you do with all that stuff? Just about everything in your home can be recycled, with a little creativity. The following are a few resourceful ways to recycle and reuse the things you no longer need.

E-waste. Most electronics, including smartphones, TVs, computers, and tablets, can be reused or recycled. It's important to be careful with any type of e-waste, though, because the objects often contain toxic chemicals such as lead, mercury, and arsenic. These chemicals can be dangerous both to the environment and to the people and animals that live in it. If you have an electronic device that still works, consider donating it before you throw it away. Give it to a local school, religious organization, or charitable agency such as Goodwill. Most computer manufacturers, such as Dell and Apple, will take back old computers once you're done using them. Stores such as Best Buy and Staples will accept used toner and ink cartridges. A few non-profit companies, including the Wireless Foundation, will accept old cell phones, batteries, and chargers. They will fix the phones and give them to people who need them.

You can set up a donation drive at your school to collect just about any type of recycling, from electronics to books to batteries.

Books, newspapers, magazines, and junk mail. Donate your used books to a local library or school if they are accepting them. Most libraries will give you a receipt that your parents can use to save money when they file their taxes. Or, you can give your books to an organization like the International Book Project, which donates them to libraries and schools in other parts of the world. You can even make money off your old books by selling them to a used bookstore or putting them up for sale (with an adult's help) online, for example, on Amazon or eBay.

Your trash company should pick up old newspapers, magazines, and mail in your recycling bins. To reduce the amount of mail that needs to be thrown away, ask your parents to call and cancel delivery of any magazines and catalogs they don't read, and have them ask junk mail companies to take your family's name off all mailing lists.

There are many ways to reuse old newspapers. You can use them to wrap fragile items before shipping them, clean your windows with them (they work like paper towels), or line the table with them while you are doing art projects.

Batteries. You have to be careful when disposing of batteries because they contain dangerous acid and other chemicals. Never throw any batteries in the trash. Bring rechargeable batteries to stores such as Office Depot and RadioShack, which will take them back. You can take alkaline batteries to your local household hazardous waste facility or to a post office that offers battery disposal services. Many auto parts stores and service centers will accept car batteries for recycling.

Automobiles. Nothing is too big to recycle, including your mother's or father's mammoth sports utility vehicle (SUV). Companies such as the American Diabetes Association and Habitat for Humanity will take cars as gifts, as well as trucks, motorcycles, boats, Jet Skis, and recreational vehicles (RVs), even if the vehicles no longer run. Plus, your parents will get a big tax deduction for their donation.

You can help nature to recycle by setting up a composting bin and using it to dispose of all your food scraps.

Food scraps. Instead of throwing your banana peels down the disposal, why not put them to good use? Starting a compost bin in your backyard will not only help get rid of food scraps, but it will also generate enough fertilizer to keep your lawn lush and green. In a compost bin, bacteria, fungi, or worms eat the waste, break things down, and release an organic fertilizer called compost.

To make a compost bin at home, put shredded

newspaper, peat moss, or sawdust into a bin. Add water to moisten it slightly. Then put about two pounds of red worms or red wigglers into the bin. Place your garbage on top. You can include refuse like coffee grounds, fruit rinds, vegetable scraps, tea bags, eggshells, and lawn clippings. Cover the bin lightly, but leave a little bit of air so that the worms can breathe. After a few weeks, you should be able to "harvest" the compost to use as fertilizer.

Other things you can recycle. Don't limit yourself to the items mentioned here. You can find a new use for just about everything in your home. Take your used shoes and clothes to the Salvation Army or one of the many other charity organizations that collect household items. Donate your broken crayon pieces to Crazy Crayons, an organization that makes new crayons out of old ones. Give your old eyeglasses to the Lions Clubs or bring them back to the store where you bought them; most stores that sell glasses will donate them for you to those in need. You can even recycle wire hangers by bringing them back to your dry cleaner.

WORKING WITH YOUR SCHOOL

Don't wait for your teachers or principal to set up a recycling program—take the first step yourself. You'd be surprised at how much you can accomplish if you set clear goals and stick to them.

GETTING CREATIVE

Is your house getting too cluttered? Try these simple projects for using objects you have around your house:

- Most of us now listen to music on our phones but still have old CDs lying around the house. Remove the CD from the clear plastic case. Insert one of your favorite photographs, and turn the empty CD case into a desktop picture frame. Or use the CDs as coasters.
- Rinse out yogurt containers. Add soil and plant seedlings to create your own windowsill herb garden.
- Tape gift wrap around the outside of a potato chip can and use the can to hold pens and pencils on your desk.
- Cut out pictures from last year's calendar to make bookmarks. To give your bookmarks more weight, cut strips from used greeting cards and tape them to the back.
- Put used dryer sheets in your dresser drawers to keep your clothes smelling fresh.
- Tape a magnet to the back of an empty raisin box and use it as a refrigerator magnet. You can also use empty candy boxes, juice boxes (just rinse them out first), bottle caps, and mint tins.
- Paint bottle caps red and black and make your own checkers game. Draw red and black squares on a piece of cardboard to use as the checkerboard.
- Save used jars or coffee containers. Fill them with homemade cookies or candy, decorate them with a bow, and give them as gifts to friends and relatives.

- Cut up used pieces of paper into small squares. Turn them over so that the clean side is showing, and put them in a pile near the phone for writing messages.
- Use paper and plastic grocery bags instead of trash bags to line your wastebaskets.
- Punch two holes about 2 inches (5 cm) from the bottom of an empty plastic soda bottle and insert a pencil to serve as a perch for birds. In your homemade bird feeder, add a few small holes slightly above the pencil so that the birds can get to the seed. Fill the soda bottle with birdseed. Use twine to tie the bird feeder to a tree branch.
- Wash an old shower curtain with hot water and disinfectant, remove the rings, and use it as a tablecloth for picnics.
- Stuff a rubber glove with ice to make an ice pack. Keep it in your freezer to use when you get injured.
- Wrap your gifts using old street or subway maps instead of decorative wrapping paper purchased at a store.

You don't have to throw away those paper bags from the grocery store. You can reuse them as trash bags.

If your school does not recycle, write up a plan—a list of activities your school can start doing now. The ideas that follow are some that you might include on your list.

- Schedule a meeting in which all the teachers can get involved and share their ideas for a school-wide recycling program.
- Establish a team made up of students and teachers to lead the recycling effort. One group of students can serve as "recycling guides," visiting classrooms and making sure that the program is running smoothly. Reward students who participate with a special party at the end of the year.

By setting up a plastics recycling program at your school, you can collect literally tons of plastics that might otherwise go into landfills or our waterways.

- Decide what items you will recycle or reuse. Your list might include paper, bottles and cans, books, school and art supplies, and sports equipment.
- Put recycling bins (especially for paper and aluminum) in every classroom. Clearly label the bins and put them right next to the trash cans so it's easy for your classmates to recycle.
- Get your fellow students excited about recycling by setting goals. If you have deposits on bottles and cans in your state, one idea is to have students aim to collect ten thousand bottles and aluminum cans to raise money for a fun school project. Or, you could encourage everyone to bring in a bag of old clothes and host a school yard sale.
- Take your list straight to the top of your school. Set up a time to present your ideas to the principal and other school administrators. Ask them how you can get your teachers and classmates involved and set a date to launch your program.

Once you have everyone in your school involved in recycling and reusing, start working on your parents and siblings. Make sure you have recycling bins at home and that everyone in your house is using them. Sit down for a family meeting to come up with new ideas for recycling and reusing. Encourage your parents to spread the word to their friends and coworkers. The more people you get involved in recycling, the bigger the positive influence you can have on your world.

TEN GREAT QUESTIONS
TO ASK YOUR SCIENCE TEACHER

1. What types of items can I recycle?
2. How does recycling help the environment?
3. Why are landfills a problem?
4. What new products are made from recycled items?
5. Is recycling really worth the time and effort?
6. Which types of recyclable items contain toxic substances?
7. How can I reuse things I have around the house?
8. How can we reuse supplies or other objects in the classroom and at school?
9. Can we plan a field trip to a local recycling center?
10. What are some recycling projects I can do at home?

GLOSSARY

biodegradable Describes a substance that can be broken down by air, water, and bacteria.

compost A process by which organic materials such as food scraps and yard waste are broken down. Compost can be used as fertilizer.

cullet Crushed, used glass that is used to make new glass.

decompose To decay or break down into parts.

ethanol A type of alcohol that can be used to power automobiles and other vehicles instead of, or in addition to, gasoline.

e-waste Televisions, smartphones, tablets, computers, video game players, and other discarded electronics equipment.

global warming An increase in the earth's temperature caused by the release of greenhouse gases (such as carbon dioxide) into the atmosphere.

incineration The process by which garbage is burned.

incinerator A furnace or container used to burn waste at very high temperatures.

landfill An area of land where trash and garbage are buried between layers of earth and special barriers to help slow leachate from running into the groundwater.

leachate Liquid that collects and runs off from the garbage in landfills.

methane A colorless, odorless, and very flammable gas that is produced as garbage decays in landfills.

pulp A soggy mass of used paper, water, and chemicals that is used to make new paper.

recycling Processing used items to turn them into something new.

reducing Using less of something.
reusing Using a product more than once.
toxic Poisonous.
vulcanization The chemical process that involves heating rubber and sulfur together to harden rubber, which also makes it difficult to recycle.

FOR MORE INFORMATION

Canadian Environmental Network (RCEN)
14 Manchester Avenue, Unit 2
Ottawa, ON K1Y 1Y9
Canada
(204) 898-6460
Website: http://www.rcen.ca
Since 1977, the Canadian Environmental Network has fostered networking among nonprofit, nongovernmental environmental organizations across Canada and internationally.

Greenpeace
702 H Street NW, Suite 300
Washington, DC 20001
(800) 722-6995
Website: http://www.greenpeace.org
Greenpeace works to organize peaceful protest and communication to educate the public about environmental problems and promote solutions.

National Recycling Coalition
727 East Washington Street
Syracuse, NY 13210
(202) 618-2107
Website: http://www.nrc-recycle.org
The members of this nonprofit group are devoted to finding new ways to recycle and reuse waste.

National Resources Defense Council
40 West 20th Street
New York, NY 10011

(212) 727-2700
Website: http://www.nrdc.org
This grassroots environmental organization helps promote green living and finds other ways to protect the environment.

Recycling and Environmental Action Planning Society (REAPS)
PO Box 444
Prince George, BC V2L 4S6
Canada
(250) 561-7327
Website: http://www.reaps.org
REAPS helps people learn about recycling, composting, and many other environmental issues.

Recycling Council of Ontario
PO Box 83
Orangeville, ON L9W 2Z5
Canada
(888) 501-9637
Website: http://www.rco.on.ca
This nonprofit agency in Canada teaches people how to reduce waste and how to get rid of waste in a more environmentally friendly way.

Sierra Club
2101 Webster Street, Suite 1300
Oakland, CA 94612
(415) 977-5500
Website: http://www.sierraclub.org

The Sierra Club was founded by legendary conservationist John Muir in 1892. It has grown into one of the nation's largest and most influential environmental groups.

FOR FURTHER READING

Baker, David. *Earth Manual: A Step-by-Step Guide to How It Works*. Sparkford, UK: Haynes Publishing, 2015.

Grinspoon, David. *Earth In Human Hands: Shaping Our Planet's Future*. New York, NY: Grand Central, 2016.

Humes, Edward. *Garbology: Our Dirty Love Affair with Trash*. New York, NY: Avery, 2013.

Kolbert, Elizabeth. *The Sixth Extinction: An Unnatural History*. New York, NY: Picador, 2015.

Macdonald, Deanna. *Eco Living Japan: Sustainable Ideas for Living Green*. Tokyo, Japan: Tuttle Publishing, 2016.

Minter, Adam. *Junkyard Planet: Travels in the Billion-Dollar Trash Trade*. New York, NY: Bloomsbury Press, 2015.

Moss, Stephen. *Planet Earth II*. London, UK: BBC Books, 2016.

Oldenziel, R., and Helmuth Trischler. *Cycling and Recycling: Histories of Sustainable Practices*. New York, NY: Berghahn, 2016.

Otfinoski, Steven. *Recycling and Upcycling: Science, Technology, Engineering*. New York, NY: Children's Press, 2016.

Paul, Miranda, and Elizabeth Zunon. *One Plastic Bag: Isatou Ceesay and the Recycling Women of the Gambia*. Minneapolis, MN: Lerner Publishing Group, 2015.

Rivera, Andrea. *Recycling*. Minneapolis, MN: Abdo Zoom, 2017.

Wilson, Edward O. *Half-Earth: Our Planet's Fight for Life*. New York, NY: Liveright Publishing Corporation, 2017.

BIBLIOGRAPHY

The Aluminum Association. "U.S. Aluminum Can Recycling Steady in 2006." June 27, 2007. http://www.aluminum.org/AM/Template.cfm?Section=Home&TEMPLATE=/CM/ContentDisplay.cfm&CONTENTID=25033.

American Chemistry Council. "Plastic Packaging Resins." Retrieved September 9, 2008. http://www.americanchemistry.com/s_plastics/bin.asp?CID=1102&DID=4645&DOC=FILE.PDF.

Benjamin, Daniel K. "Recycling Rubbish: Eight Great Myths About Waste Disposal." *PERC Reports*, Volume 21, September 2003. http://www.perc.org/articles/article224.php.

Blatt, Harvey. *America's Environmental Report Card: Are We Making the Grade?* Cambridge, MA: MIT Press, 2005.

Breyer, Melissa. "Trash By the Numbers: Startling Statistics About US Garbage." TreeHugger. September 12, 2017. https://www.treehugger.com/environmental-policy/trash-numbers-startling-statistics-about-americans-and-their-garbage.html.

California Environmental Protection Agency. "The Illustrated History of Recycling." Retrieved August 4, 2008. http://www.p2pays.org/ref/26/25070.pdf.

Cothran, Helen, ed. *Garbage and Recycling:* Farmington Hills, MI: Greenhaven Press, 2003.

Deneen, Sally. "How to Recycle Practically Anything." *E—The Environmental Magazine*, May/June 2006, Vol. 17, p. 26–32.

Ellick, Adam B. "Houston Resists Recycling, and Independent Streak Is Cited." *New York Times*, July 29, 2008. http://www.nytimes.com.

Energy Information Administration. "Energy Kid's Page." Retrieved July 10, 2008. http://eia.doe.gov/kids/energyfacts/saving/recycling/solidwaste/recycling.html.

Green Media Group. *Greenopia, New York City: The Definitive Guide to More Than 1,300 Eco-Friendly Business and Resources*. Berkeley, CA: Green Media Group, 2008.

HowStuffWorks. "How Recycling Works." Retrieved August 1, 2008. http://www.howstuffworks.com/recycling.htm.

Keep America Beautiful. "Waste Reduction." Retrieved August 1, 2008. http://www.kab.org.

Nakazawa, Liz. "A New Corn-Based Plastic Disappears Into the Dirt." September 4, 2003. http://www.csmonitor.com.

National Geographic. "A Whopping 91% of Plastic Isn't Recycled." July 19, 2017. http://news.nationalgeographic.com/2017/07/plastic-produced-recycling-waste-ocean-trash-debris-environment.

National Recycling Coalition. "Top 10 Reasons to Recycle." Retrieved July 10, 2008. http://www.nrc-recycle.org/top10reasonstorecycle.aspx.

Small, Meredith F. "Real-World Recycling Puts U.S. to Shame." Yahoo! News. August 23, 2008. http://news.yahoo.com.

Tierney, John. "Recycling Is Garbage." *New York Times*, June 30, 1996. http://www.nytimes.com.

US Environmental Protection Agency. "Advancing Sustainable Materials Management: Facts and Figures." August 10, 2017. https://www.epa.gov/smm/advancing-sustainable-materials-management-facts-and-figures.

US Environmental Protection Agency. "Batteries." Retrieved August 5, 2008. http://www.epa.gov/garbage/battery.htm.

US Environmental Protection Agency. "Combustion." Retrieved September 4, 2008. http://www.epa.gov/epaoswer/education/quest/pdfs/unit2/chap4/u2-4_combustion.pdf.

US Environmental Protection Agency. "eCycling." Retrieved August 5, 2008. http://www.epa.gov/epaoswer/hazwaste/recycle/ecycling/basic.htm.

US Environmental Protection Agency. "Municipal Solid Waste Generation, Recycling, and Disposal in the United States: Facts and Figures for 2006." Retrieved August 5, 2008. http://www.epa.gov/msw/msw99.htm.

US Environmental Protection Agency. "Resource Conservation and Recovery Act." Retrieved August 21, 2008. http://epa.gov/superfund/students/clas_act/haz-ed/ff_06.htm.

US Environmental Protection Agency. "Reuse + Recycling=Waste Reduction: A Guide for Schools and Groups." Retrieved September 20, 2008. http://www.epa.gov/epaoswer/osw/students/school.pdf.

Wald, Matthew L. "Gassing Up with Garbage." *New York Times*, July 24, 2008. http://www.nytimes.com.

Washington State Department of Ecology. "Kids Recycle Page." Retrieved July 10, 2008. http://www.ecy.wa.gov/programs/swfa/kidspage.

Zeller, Tom. "Recycling the Big Picture." *National Geographic*, January 2008, Vol. 213, pp. 82–87.

INDEX

U

V

W

ABOUT THE AUTHORS

Nicholas Faulkner is a writer living in New Jersey.

Stephanie Watson is a regular contributor to several online and print health and science publications. She has written or contributed to multiple books, including *Biotechnology: Changing Life Through Science* and *Critical Perspectives on Pollution* (Scientific American Critical Anthologies on Environment and Climate). She lives in Atlanta, Georgia.

PHOTO CREDITS

Cover Robert Daly/Caiaimage/Getty Images; pp. 4–5 (background) namtipStudio/Shutterstock.com; p. 5 Billy Hustace/Photographer's Choice/Getty Images; pp. 7, 17 29, 41 monticello/Shutterstock .com; p. 8 Muellek Josef/Shutterstock.com; p. 11 Marquisphoto /Shutterstock.com; pp. 14–15 Dalibor Danilovic/Shutterstock .com; p. 18 spwidoff/Shutterstock.com; p. 20 DarioEgidi/E+/Getty Images; p. 23 Huguette Roe/Shutterstock.com; p. 26 Neirfy /Shutterstock.com; p. 27 asiseeit/E+/Getty Images; pp. 30–31 Dougal Waters/DigitalVision/Getty Images; pp. 34, 38 © AP Images; pp. 36–37 Wolfgang Kaehler/LightRocket/Getty Images; p. 42 fstop123/E+/Getty Images; p. 44 cjp/E+/Getty Images; p. 47 Eternity in an Instant/The Image Bank/Getty Images; p. 48 AP Photo/Couer d'Alene Press, Jerome A. Pollos.

Design: Michael Moy; Photo Research: Karen Huang